THE GHOST STORIES OF TERRELL, TEXAS

A COLLECTION OF TRUE AND AMAZING HAUNTINGS TOLD

BY PARANORMAL INVESTIGATORS.

BRENDA NEWBY

Co-Authored by Mary Jo Woodruff

THE GHOST STORIES OF TERRELL, TEXAS: A COLLECTION OF TRUE AND AMAZING HAUNTINGS AS TOLD BY PARANORMAL INVESTIGATORS

We have tried, to the best of our abilities, to write these stories regarding events, locales, and conversations strictly from memory. To protect anonymity, some information, including the names of specific locations and details about individuals, may be changed to protect personal privacy. All efforts have been taken to prevent adaptation of the actual experience described to us. All labors are made to tell the stories relayed to us as carefully and with as much accuracy as possible.

Cover designed by Brenda Newby and Mary Jo Woodruff

All photographs were taken by Mary Jo Woodruff

For information contact:

Brenda Newby at https://www.terrellghosts.com

Dedication

To my mother and my husband, Mary Jo and Jason. You kept the business from failing even when my body had other plans. You also managed to keep me in the physical world. Neither was an easy feat, but you both rose to the almost impossible challenge. I owe you my life.

To my son, Dayton: There are no words to express how you have made my life complete. Lead by example and not by words. Always aim to live with transparency, honesty, and integrity. Be the best you can be, not to serve your ego but to serve others.

Many years from now, after I have left the physical world, please search for me. Listen for the word, "Carnegie." I will be there. If you pass before me, I will listen for the same. If instead I hear you exclaim, "Tag! You're it!" I will cease further communication.

Contents

WHY IS THE CITY SO HAUNTED? 5

MAGNETIC ENERGY FROM THE RAILROAD 13

LEY LINE PROXIMITY 17

POSITIVE MEMORIES FROM THE DEPARTED 18

THE AWNING COLLAPSE 20

THE IRIS THEATRE 23

BOOKS AND CRANNIES 31

THE CARNEGIE LIBRARY 39

THE BRITISH FLYING TRAINING SCHOOL 49

THE WARREN BUILDING 55

THE TRAIN DEPOT 61

THE BRIN BUILDING 68

CAUTION: AREA MAY HAVE MOVING OBJECTS 71

NOW I SEE YOU, NOW I DON'T: THE APPARITIONS 74

THE DEPARTED HAVE A SENSE OF HUMOR TOO 78

TERRELL STATE HOSPITAL 81

THE ANDERSON BUILDING 90

SPIRITUAL YIN AND YANG 93

LOOK TWICE 94

She Needed A Name... 95
Dancing Orbs 97
One Fateful Fall Brings a Difficult Decision 100
Enter the Angel 103
Does the Nurse Still Reside in Anderson? 105
A Visit from Lizzie? 107
THE MEDIUMS 109
They Walk Among Us 110
Using Mediums as an Investigative Tool: 112
The Accidental Ouija Board Test 114
Unseen Eyes Watching Our Tour 115
Medium Impressions in Terrell's Haunted Buildings 117
Mediums Abound at the Headquarters 118
A Picture Finds Its Home 120
CONCLUSION 123
WORKS CITED 128
ACKNOWLEDGMENTS 131
ABOUT THE AUTHOR 132
THE CO-AUTHOR 134

1

Why is the City so Haunted?

"Every city is a ghost. New buildings rise upon the bones of the old so that each shiny steel beam, each tower of brick carries within it the memories of what has gone before, an architectural haunting. Sometimes you can catch a glimpse of these former incarnations in the awkward angle of a street or a filigreed gate, an old oak door peeking out from a new façade, the plaque commemorating the spot that was once a battleground, which became a saloon. "

-Libba Bray, Lair of Dreams

THROUGHOUT THE YEARS TERRELL HAS had an ever-changing landscape of businesses along Moore Avenue. Similar cities have underground tunnels, and we confirmed this ourselves by finding the barricaded entrances. Rumors exist there could be as much as 3 miles of winding underpasses, and we understand they served the town's bank, infirmary, and the state-run psychiatric hospital which we will discuss later.

Coincidentally, these buildings have significant reports of paranormal activity. Most Terrellites are oblivious to the existence of these tunnels. However, these infrastructures were common in historic, developed areas and served a variety of purposes. Many towns used these tunnels for running moonshine and often helped slaves in their escape from the barbaric practices of their masters. Years later, the passageways became the secret playground for the local children. Many of our tour guests had waned nostalgic about exploring the underground city when they were young.

At some point during the early 19th century, Terrell was quite a busy, upscale city. Older residents fondly remember Moore Avenue as being a lively street packed with culture and activity for everyone. Throughout the years there have been Opera Houses, billiard halls, general stores, candy stores, and even wagon shops. As well, we've spoken about the many soda shops where the younger residents spent time socializing. They could also be found in one of the many movie theaters there. During the years of Prohibition, there were a few "underground" places where someone might grab a drink at a local Speakeasy. If a gentleman needed a little company for the evening, it could easily be arranged if you went to the east side of Highway 34, so we have heard.

The top floors of the Anderson building were rumored to have its share of card games where it's alleged the city's newspaper had been bet in a single hand of five card stud. Whether it was lost or won depended on what you held in your final hand when the cards hit the table. There are stories likened to anything you could relate to the days of the Old West. Indeed, if you were determined enough, you could find some old bones buried a little less deep then originally due to soil erosion. There is no shortage of wild legends and big stories here. I'm not sure what is truly real or just a tall tale. In the end, does it really matter? These stories make a small town more enjoyable. One remarkable thing about all cities as charming as Terrell is having a little colorful past only makes it more intriguing generations later. However, we are most interested in a different sort of story here. The stories we have can't be looked up on microfiche or Googled. We want to know more about the things that go bump in the night and send a chill up your spine. As curious beings, we want to hear about those things which make us question ourselves and what we just saw.

We are here for the ghosts and things that cannot be explained. In a city with as many paranormal stories as Terrell you are drawn to the historic buildings with the hope you might encounter something that convinces you of the existence of life after death. It wasn't until the recent few years when I became convinced of such things, this after my first paranormal experience. It was an unexplainable photograph captured by my mother, in my presence, around my 36th birthday. The picture was taken in another small city not too far from Terrell. Initially, I did not discover Terrell for its ghost stories. In fact, I found Terrell in a manner which was not paranormal at all.

As most typical "bridezillas" do before she weds her groom to be, she becomes hysterically aware of each intimate detail of the day to be. So much so, her best maid even has thoughts of possibly smothering her to death with a pillow during her slumber rather than continue to subject herself to the insistent complaining. Despite repeated proclamations, I would never become this woman, Now I can shamefully admit, I went incredibly bonkers before the big day and very loudly and obscenely about my displeasure something wasn't quite the way I wanted. My obsession had become out of hand. My mother seized the moment and used it as a segue to make me aware of the mustache steadily growing above my upper lip for the past few years. Yet another curse of being over a certain age for a woman whether I wanted to admit it or not. Now was the time something had to be done about it. No longer able to cry oblivion it was decided walking down the aisle sporting a Fu Manchu was unacceptable. Discreetly, my mother made an appointment to see a highly recommended electrolysis technician in Terrell.

The clinic is still on the main stretch of downtown. Driving down the Farm to Market Road 148, I would turn onto State Highway 80 where it converts to a more intimate section of road, dotted with intersections, and stop lights. No longer was it a highway but a comfortable stretch of street, Moore Avenue. This area is lined with buildings built from as early as the 1800s and still possess a historic charm despite man's attempt to modernize them. This area is home to the Small Business District. Today the street is lined with an array of unique shopping opportunities to suit almost any person's taste. It is an area that demands to be noticed even by the most unobservant traveler. Despite my overwhelming anxiety about the procedure ahead of me, there was an awareness of an immediate and sudden heaviness to the air after crossing the intersection at Rockwall Avenue I have never felt to be "sensitive" or "psychic "in any way, but now I quickly recognize the sensation well. I would later learn this is a sign of being in the presence of spirit energy. At that moment, the heaviness was so perceptible that my anxiety left, and I was soon overwhelmed by calmness. Years after that experience, I learned many people are easily able to sense these ghosts of the past. Mediums, who are more common than you realize, may be able to hear, see, feel, and even smell these energetic signatures put out by ghosts. These skills I have never been able to tap into, but I can easily recognize atmospheric shifts in the air. If that shift is strong enough, my old and worn out joints may scream like Aunt Edna's "trick" knee. We all know Aunt Edna was more reliable than David Finfrock, our most trusted Dallas meteorologist. Future trips into the area produced the same results. It seemed at the crossing of Rockwall Avenue at Moore Avenue this palpable sensation would at once consume me. It never occurred to me this might have paranormal or ghostly origins. At the time, I only considered ghosts a vague possibility but with most stories coming from products of over-imagination and nothing more. There has never been a sense of negativity in the area. Instead, it was like stepping back to a simpler time. I always thought, "If these buildings could only talk, the stories they could tell." Something as different about this part of the city, and the number of unexplainable experiences told by those who frequented there soon began to seem less of a coincidence. Eventually, I had a paranormal experience that happened far from Moore Avenue, but it launched me to investigate the area further. As I became more intrigued, soon after my own paranormal experience, I became a bit of a paranormal hobbyist. As my skills developed as an investigator with a professionally assembled team, we begin to focus on Terrell. We all started to theorize several opinions for the substantial number of accounts about perceived paranormal events in that area.

THE SMALL BUSINESS DISTRICT

OF TERRELL, TEXAS

Photograph from Moore Avenue as you cross into the small business district. The buildings in this area are historic, most being built in the late 1800s.

Magnetic Energy from the Railroad

Many Investigators believe our departed loved ones feed off energy sources such as magnetic, static, atmospheric, and electromagnetic, energy to help themselves manifest in different manners. If they can channel this energy effectively, then it increases the chances they can be seen, heard, and sometimes even move objects usually to the complete shock of unsuspecting witnesses. Ironically, the railroad track running parallel to the small business district on Moore Avenue is less than one city block away from the busiest street in town. At one time, the team was subletting space in the Brin Building in the area. One evening, I was painfully behind on my work, I spent a restless night at the office intending to start in the wee morning hours. Also, staying overnight in the building supplied the best opportunity to observe ghostly activity when it was at its most quiet. Lying on my air mattress that evening, I had been awoken to the train passing through almost twenty times. That's a hell of a lot of magnetic energy thrown into the air, and it is no surprise that night was particularly busy at the office for ghostly activity, too. The train generated so much energy that at times our equipment would be sitting out and our proximity meters would light up and beep shortly after it would pass through. Sometimes the intensity of the train would be so strong the building would shake and vibrate. You can physically feel the tremor in the center of your body as the horn blares warning the intersection as it steadfastly approaches. Each time that train came through it was one of the most amazing and fulfilling sensations I have ever felt as it was a reminder of the historical commerce the train brought here in the early century allowing the city to thrive and grow. It is a sensation of achievement, innovation, and arduous work. It is also an unending supply of magnetic energy for our ghostly predecessors to harness and make themselves known.

Tak, a Psychic Medium we worked with, once asked me if the rails would close when there was no train. I had never experienced that before. He laughed and almost seemed unsure of himself. He said, "I feel as if there is a ghost train zooming through the city sometimes." The next morning, I gasped as I watched the rails close on their own and sat there for 5 minutes with no train in sight. Since then, I have heard several reports of this phenomenon happening in Terrell. I wonder what the host train's freight is: Cargo or Passengers

THE RAILROAD TRACKS RUNNING BEHIND THE SMALL BUSINESS DISTRICT

Could there be a ghost train that travels down these railroad tracks? Magnetic energy is said to power paranormal activity. One assumption is this is why there are so many ghost stories in this haunted town.

Ley Line Proximity

Moore Avenue is rumoured as being immediately in the center of two parallel ley lines. Many people may have heard of ley lines but are still unsure of what they are. There is a lot of mystery and intrigue surrounding these migratory paths. It is difficult for me to wrap my own mind around these gateways, but I will do my best to describe them as I understand them. The concept is quite complex, and the scientific theory is still debatable, ley lines are alleged invisible lines that connect places of spiritual or religious significance. This may include sites such as Stonehenge or Easter Island. The theory is still controversial, but some believe ley lines have electromagnetic energy that is measurable by meters and individual animals, including humans but primarily birds, are sensitive to them. One current concept is related to a tissue found in the Ethmoid sinuses of many animals known to draw them into alignment with migratory paths. I'm not sure how much science is currently behind this idea and what its consequence is on Terrell, but many paranormal investigators share a certainty that these areas have increased paranormal activity both at the lines themselves as well as where they intersect.

Although I never tried to locate an intersection in

the city I have discovered through documented research, Moore Avenue appears to reside in a parallel relationship with the lines. It is easy for a believer to deduce the increase in ghostly events may have something to do with Moore Avenue's placement on the planet itself. This theory is still far out for some people, but I believe it should be considered. Few people debate the level of paranormal activity, ghost sightings, and other unusual experiences in the city. I often told our previous tour guests, "I could more easily list places in Terrell that are not haunted as opposed to places that are haunted. To list the haunted areas would simply take me all day."

Positive Memories from the Departed

I think that many souls simply don't want to leave the city. Considering the stories and letters written by the boys from the No. 1 British Flying Training School, also known as the BFTS, discussed later in this book, the Terrellites must believe they are still there today. Possibly, inhabiting one of the many former soda shops or one of the many movie theatres that were in operation then. These were places of much-needed socialization for the airborne soldiers, and they often wrote of the teenage antics that went on between themselves and the local girls in town. A common theme for these boys, according to these letters, is that they all wanted to return to Terrell after the war.

Even today, the small business owners and the city's residents are always planning improvements to the town. There is a magic in the air I believe comes from the people here and those who have been there in the past too. The further we have delved into the city's history, the more we've learned about kindness, citizenship, and honor of Terrell's people. It was easy to understand that this place would be hard to leave. Leaving due to the experience of death would be no exception. Therefore, we selected this city to develop and run local ghost tours. It is an undervalued and undiscovered city full of history and ghosts who many believe still visit their former hometown. We are honored to tell the stories of the spirits we think are still here. I hope that my great-grandchildren will be telling stories of our paranormal team decades from now while we thump and knock on the walls with delight and slam doors for the bewilderment of ghost tour guests. We're going to have some fun with them.

2

The Awning Collapse

"There is a saying in Tibetan, 'Tragedy should be utilized as a source of strength.' No matter what sort of difficulties, how painful experience is, if we lose our hope, that's our real disaster."

Dalai Lama XIV

IT WAS NOVEMBER IN THE YEAR OF 1884, and it began as a beautiful, festive day. Families were gathering picnic lunches and blankets to sit on. The ladies wore wide-brimmed hats to keep the sun off their skin, as was the style then. Today was the day that the Sells Brother's circus came to town. They started the festivities by parading the circus performers down Moore Avenue. It was a great day and is even expressed by a new mural painted on the side of the former Brin Opera House.

Over 500 spectators gathered along Moore Avenue, and the sun beat down on the viewers. The men decided that it would be beneficial to place the women and children underneath the awnings, fashioned like verandas, that donned the stores to keep them shaded. To make room for them, the men gathered atop the sturdy coverings allowing for a great view while keeping their families out of the direct sun and heat.

It was just after 10:00 A.M., there were at least 100 men on top of the canopies before the unthinkable happened (The New York Times). One of the wooden awnings collapsed completely trapping an unknown number of women and children underneath. The iron rods that held up the building in front of the Mississippi Dry Goods store, owned by Morris Brin, fell into the windows and the roof partially collapsed. Individuals were caught below the rubble. The fall from above resulted in other causalities. At least 4 were killed at the scene, and 75 were severely hurt, some fatally, during the accident (McCarty). Those in need of aid were taken into the closest businesses for treatment. As a testament to the heroism of those involved, even the parading circus participants jumped into action to assist led by Allen Sells, the circus owner. As well, the spectators on the other side of the street ran to help. (Indiana) Local newspapers provided a partial list of those affected. Some were noted to have fatal injuries, but there is no definitive list of those that perished or survived. The children that were involved were not listed by name, only those adults with a notation that a child was with the victim. (Indiana). At the time, there was no hospital in Terrell, and many of those that attended the parade were from neighboring towns. Complete records were difficult, if not impossible, to keep.

Witness reports of child apparitions are abundant in the small business district. We assume that one of the reasons we have so many stories may be because of this tragic day. Child spirits are so prevalent in the locations discussed in this book; it is impossible to keep up with each story. Most buildings have at least one report of a child spirit. It is pure speculation the awning collapse could be a possibility of these reports.

The apparition, Lizzie, that we discuss so much through the remainder of this book may or may not be involved in this unfortunate incident.

3

The Iris Theatre

"I have the terrible feeling that, because I am wearing a white beard and am sitting in the back of the theatre, you expect me to tell you the truth about something. These are the cheap seats, not Mount Sinai."

-Orson Welles

TWO OF THE LOVELIEST PEOPLE YOU HAVE ever met own what is often considered the heart of the small business district. Within this epicenter lies three businesses: The Silhouette Resale Shop, Books and Crannies, and The Iris Theater. Undoubtedly, this is one of the most active places I have seen as far as the paranormal is concerned. Thankfully, the spirits that live here seem to be as pleasant and benevolent as the people who own it.

The Iris Theatre is a black box theatre, which is a venue with black walls, black ceilings, dark floors, and stadium chairs, that allow for a small audience. This theatre seats 34 people and is home to productions by the Terrell-based group, Vagabond Players, who perform community theatre productions several times a year. The small, dark theatre gives you a sense of being anywhere the actors take you. As someone who has seen many plays in this theatre, the result is quite useful. As a paranormal investigator, I can tell you that theatres tend to be a hotspot for ghosts and hauntings and the Iris is no exception.

The building was opened as a movie theatre in the 1920s. It continued to operate as a movie theatre until around 2001. The current owners remodeled the building to include three separate spaces. The traditional bookstore and clothing consignment areas fill about three-fourths of the space, with the black box theatre built across the width of the remaining space at the back. The entrance to the theatre is covered by a black velvet drape, and when first stepping into the area, your eyes must adjust to the darkness. Witnesses entering the dark space say they have seen a white, smoky apparition, believed to be a former owner and caretaker of the movie theatre. They say he sits at the very top of the ascending theatre seats on the far stage right side. People report it appears as if the specter is looking down upon the patrons and actors as if to oversee the theatre. Witnesses state he wears a plaid shirt and sits silently, completely being unaware or uninterested in anyone who enters and moves around in the theater. He simply is there for his own reasons, which, will never be known to us. Others have professed to capture photographs of the smoky apparition as he sits quietly in his chosen spot.

All three businesses give you a sense of being at home. There has been more than one occasion in which I nodded off, completely relaxed, in that theatre during an event because the atmosphere is so calming. Despite the welcoming feeling, I always must minimize my time spent there since I am overly sensitive to barometric pressure changes. It is impossible for me to ignore the severe drop in barometric pressure as soon as I cross the black-curtained barrier into the theatre. If the spirits must use whatever sources they can to access manifestation, barometric pressure must be a resource for them. Never has such a drop in pressure been more clear to me than in this theatre. Although it has never been measured by me, personally, there is a discernible change in the air pressure. The longer I stay in the theatre, the heavier it becomes, and others have reported the same sensation.

We often have events in the theatre, including group readings done by our talented mediums. It makes for an intense and incredible venue to host such intimate experiences due to its size and dark surroundings. I recall one instance when Medium, Amy Scott, was conducting a group reading. She was speaking to a woman who had been complaining of a mysterious presence when she moved into her home. Amy was explaining that the man was attached to an object that belonged to her brother and that he was upset about the move and harbored feelings of anger towards her brother even in death. She told the lady that he shouldn't be trusted, and the best thing she could do would be to identify the object he was attached to, remove it from the property. After that, the resident should speak to him and tell him he was no longer appreciated there. She should be clear he would need to seek another place to haunt. It was at this point the cat, Maddie, the feline that occupies the store, jumped from her regular spot in a hurry, and darted out of the room. As well, our two Boxers with us that evening were sitting in the top row. These dogs are very well trained and ignore most everything unless we give them permission to investigate something. Suddenly, they both started to whimper, and the female Boxer begins to hide under the seat next to her while crying loudly. At that moment, the woman who was in the exchange with Amy about the angry presence in her home felt an unseen hand force a glass of wine, held in her hand, dumping it down the entire front of her blouse.

Another unique event that happened at the Iris Theatre is foreign interference with our electronic investigative equipment. One instance occurred during a routine investigation.

Protocol before an investigation includes fresh batteries in all the equipment and full recharging for those items with rechargeable batteries. We also carry backup equipment, still and video cameras, and audio recorders. On this occasion, the photographer entered the theatre and began shooting photos, working counterclockwise around the space. The standard process is to take three to five still shots of each view, methodically working around the area. Just a few frames into the shoot, the digital camera's battery died. She brought in the backup camera, a smaller megapixel, but a camera that has captured many anomalies over a few years. And after a short time, that battery died, too. Not to be shorthanded, the photographer goes to her car and brings out a camera she keeps in the car for impromptu photographs, fully charged. There were few photographs taken of the Iris that day, because the third camera's battery did not last long, either. It seemed the very air in the theatre was absorbing the stored energy. There were numerous photos of the bookstore and consignment shop that day, including some anomalies, but the spirits in the Iris were having none of it.

On another day, the photographer was tending both an audio recorder and a video recorder during a medium group reading in the theatre. Both devices appeared to be recording, all the lights and bells were indicating full operation. However, later in the office, we realized the video recorder captured approximately the first minute of the session, while the audio recorder more, about two minutes. Although it is quite easy to explain many events away when they occur alone, there has never been a solid organic explanation for all the failures.

If you are curious about the spirits of the Iris Theatre, you can visit and experience the venue for yourself. The Vagabond Players perform several times a year, and the Iris presents classic movies for free a couple Friday nights each month. You can visit www.bookscrannies.com and hit the Iris Theatre tab to see a current schedule and sign up for the email list of the upcoming movies and plays. The spirits and owners would enjoy a visit from you. The price of admission is far reasonable for the tremendous fun you will have.

THE IRIS THEATRE

The black box theatre where it is reported a man watches over the audience and productions onstage. The Iris Theatre is home to productions given by the Vagabond Players.

4

Books and Crannies

"Do you really want to know where we come from?" she said. "In every century, in every country, they'll call us something different. They'll say we're ghosts, angels, demons, elemental spirits, and giving us a name doesn't help anybody. When did a name change what someone is?"

=Brenna Yovanoff, The Replacement

ONE WOULD BE AS LIKELY TO CAPTURE a photograph of Chupacabra and Big Foot having high noon tea than finding a real bookstore. One of the few left lies in the heart of downtown Terrell: Books and Crannies. It is the cornerstone of the small business community there and is almost a hub for information about the rest of the town.

I've seen many a traveler come by to find out where they could find a specific place in the city. I attribute that to the inviting energy that rolls out the door and the grand Iris marquis that draws you to the entrance of the store. The books are not organized in the usual fashion of horizontal arrangement but vertically stacked in almost a whimsical style. There is also a 'method to the madness' sorting system that any of the staff will gladly guide you through. Books and Crannies has been designed for faithful readers who consume books left and right and is unique to any traditional big store found everywhere else. The store throws caution to the wind with unique shelf displays where books fit into bright white shelves adorned with arches above the aisles. Other aisles have the added allure of beautiful black velvet curtains to divide sections. As any delightful bookstore should, it has chairs and comfy sitting places strategically placed to make it easy for a reading aficionado to sort through their finds. You suddenly feel at home. There is always a quiet, private spot to duck into if you need to get lost in a few pages. The current owners won't mind a bit if you sit a spell, drink some coffee, and thumb through a novel. All who work there are quiet as librarians but just ask a question, and they are jumping to their feet to help you find what you want.

The owner, Gayle, has spoken to me about the

times she senses an invisible hand gently and endearingly stroke her arm or hair or hears her name softly called from the back of the store. She perceives the contact as kind and protective. She has absolutely no fear of the resident spirits and is quite protective of them.

I recall a story she shared with me about a paranormal investigation team who expressed irritation with the lack of ghostly interaction during an investigation. One investigator displayed a bit of arrogance and, to no surprise, the study was yielding no results. To elicit some response from the other side, the investigator spoke out loudly to the room, "If you give us some indication that you are here, we will pack up our stuff and leave." Seconds later, a book flew off the shelf and launched itself towards the investigator. Excited, the team continued with a barrage of questions. The owner looked up and said, "You told them you would leave if they responded. They did as you asked. You need to be true to your word and leave." The team was dismissed. Like many of Moore Avenue's small business owners, Gayle is a living spokesperson for those who may not be heard as clearly.

As paranormal investigators, we do our best to make sure they are treated with the same dignity they were offered while in physical form. These are people we are dealing with, and they should be treated with courtesy.

The bookstore is extraordinarily busy with spirit activity. It is not unusual for a book to suddenly launch itself off the shelf. In some instances, it might appear to fly in a sudden 90° angle down the aisle. I recount a personal episode during the intermission of the Vagabond Player's "Steel Magnolias." I had walked to the lady's room, and my husband had stopped to pick up a large and heavy book on firearms. He replaced the book and met me at the front of the store, and we stopped for a bag of popcorn, freshly popped in an old fashion machine. Refreshments are provided with no expected charge, but donations are appreciated as they are used to raise money for the local animal shelter. Yet another example of how the business community gives back to others.

Upon approaching the threshold of the theater, we stopped to investigate a loud sound behind us. As we turned, we witnessed the firearms book my husband held in his hands only a few minutes earlier being launched, by some unseen force, across the aisle where it hit the opposing bookshelf. The book had flown at least 5 feet, and it was done with intention and purpose. There was so much strength behind this movement that it caused several books on the opposite shelf to fall to the ground.

Immediately, I knew someone was trying to get my attention. Days earlier, our team's medium and I had visited the store. This could have easily been a random event, or maybe the spirit recognized me? Even though we were initially startled, I chuckled and said out loud, "Thank you for remembering me. It is great to see you again so soon." I understand that this is common in Books and Crannies and is just one example of many paranormal experiences that take place.

Books and Crannies often rescues a cat to live out his or her life among the stacks at the store. I can imagine that this would be one cushy job for any cat. The customers often bring the store's cat toys, treats, and luxury items. I've been guilty of indulging the bookstore cat myself from time to time. What's a little catnip among friends, right?

Years ago, a black tortoiseshell, named Satchamo was the mascot of Books and Crannies. Sadly, Satchamo advanced to the Rainbow Bridge, and a new feline, a Hurricane Katrina rescue named Maddie, took over the role. One day the owner approached me at the front door performing the dance of a small child needing a bathroom trip. I knew that she was excited and must have a juicy new ghost story for me. She did! At this point, I joined her in her dance. She told me of a little girl who had been in earlier that week with her mother. The little girl had played with Maddie, the resident cat at the time, and she told Gayle she tried to catch the black cat, but it ran through the curtains of the theater threshold before she could catch him. The black cat had become shrouded in the darkness of the theater and couldn't be found. When the owner said she didn't have a black cat, the little girl was adamant that there were two cats: Maddie, and a cat fitting the description of Satchamo!

I am deeply saddened to say that we recently lost Maddie. Personally, I do not have a fondness for cats. However, Maddie was different from most. I can tell you that there was something special about this feline. She was a cat for all the people, and she always played like a kitten to our amusement. Her eyes followed objects that we couldn't see. Being startled and running out of an area extraordinarily quickly as if something unseen had grabbed her tail was common for Maddie and always gave us a giggle. What could she see that we did not? We often rented the Iris Theater for our mediums' group sessions, Maddie would always come and set up front as if in honor of the spirits. Often, she would sit on the stage, back turned to the audience, and watch the dark wall towards the front of the room. Maddie will be deeply missed.

Now, I would be remiss not to tell a story of a friend

who had his own experience in the Silhouette Resale Shop, which quickly made him a believer in the spirit world. Richard is a kind man, but he was damn near 7-foot-tall and not the kind of stranger you'd want to meet in a back alley alone. He always had a Glock 45 strapped to his hip, and he knew how to use it. He was a frequent attendant of our ghost tours and always welcome to attend as he enjoyed the tours and was a good friend. Richard was in the restroom that evening, and he quickly was converted from non-believer to believer. As he stood there, pants dropped to his ankles, he felt a sudden pressure as if someone was gently pushing the inside of this calves, and then the sensation started to run right up his thighs! Well, everyone got the laugh of a lifetime as our tall, brave, friend quickly appeared, almost sans pants, running out the restroom door yelling and screaming like a teenage girl. To the Spirits of the resale shop: Well played

BOOKS AND CRANNIES

Books often fly off of the shelves as if someone throws them. We witnessed this happen during a visit to the bookstore. It was so hard that it made a loud noise and knocked books down on the shelf across from it.

5

THE CARNEGIE LIBRARY

"We had quite enough snobbery in this world without exporting it to the hereafter."

-Rick Riordan
The Throne of Fire

THE CARNEGIE LIBRARY WAS BUILT IN 1904 with funds donated by steel tycoon Andrew Carnegie. Over 2500 libraries worldwide were donated by this businessman and philanthropist who believed education was the key to success. Many of these libraries no longer exist, and those that are still standing have been repurposed as museums or other displays of historical significance. (Wikipedia) The Carnegie grant came with the city assuming responsibility for maintenance, operations, and content. It was during the 1980s that Terrell built a new city library and the Carnegie building became the Terrell Heritage

Museum. Today it is supported and operated by the Terrell Heritage Society (THS).

The building is beautifully designed and typical of all Carnegie libraries in that it is a two-story structure with an entrance that opens into a foyer, presenting two beautiful staircases. The top floor has two offices at the front of the building, a large open auditorium with a slightly elevated stage, a closet at stage right, and a closet at stage left with stairs to the bottom floor. The bottom floor of the museum is one large room with two smaller rooms to each side at the rear of the building, each side with a separate small bathroom under the staircases. Hardwood floors adorn the building. It is a testament to the grandeur of buildings of the time.

On one occasion, two volunteers were working at a table in the front room. One of the volunteers flinched as she saw something unusual that seemed to come from the direction of the foyer. She asked her companion, "Did you just see that?" Her reply was simply, "No." The volunteer described what she had just witnessed. She saw what appeared to be an average size, dark, 3-dimensional, human shadow walking across the interior threshold into the foyer. The spirit moved quickly and with unknown purpose or intention. We were told several stories about this shadowed figure by other witnesses.

One of our investigators professes her own story of the man presenting as a shadow silhouette cast upon the foyer wall one day when she was volunteering. On occasion, when the figure manifested as a shadow, the door chimes would ring as if someone had entered the foyer. The volunteer/greeter for the day would walk to the entrance to greet the guest only to find that no one had come in. On some days, the chimes would ring mysteriously so often that the museum attendants would unplug them.

This type of door chime always makes a fantastic and inexpensive investigation tool. These devices are called passive infrared chimes or IR sensors. Purchased at any hardware store, they are economic tools that should be in every paranormal investigator's kit. The term infrared is used to describe the spectrum of light that exists just above the view of human vision. This infrared layer of light also has a temperature signature. Once the sensor is in place, it records the ambient temperature on the surface of the object it is pointed at. If anything with a different temperature crosses the infrared beam, it alerts by ringing the chime. Shadows will not falsely set off the chime as they do not have a temperature signature. Perhaps, the shadow man reported in the foyer of the Carnegie caused a temperature change? I guess we will never know the answer, but if the chimes are going off during his movement, then we must hypothesize that this is the case.

The noises of the Carnegie building are also quite significant and unnerving. A person would not expect to hear such loud sounds when you are alone in a quiet building. Footsteps can sometimes be heard moving across the original hardwood floor that still exists on second-floor level. At times, it sounds like the footsteps are descending the staircase on either side. The men's restroom door sounds as if it is opening and closing on its own accord. One volunteer told us that she was sitting at the museum one morning, accompanied by her husband that day. She was busy sweeping the floor near the double doors at the front of the building. Her husband was sitting at the downstairs table quietly reading the paper only a few feet away from her. At that moment, she heard the unmistakable sound as someone entered and shut the door to the men's room. She automatically assumed that her husband had gotten up to visit the men's room. At least, she thought that was the case until she looked behind her to see her husband just as he was before, quietly sitting and reading the paper. He hadn't moved one inch from where she had left him minutes earlier. She inquired if he had gotten up to go to the bathroom and he simply said that he hadn't moved. Do apparitions need to occasionally relieve themselves too? I guess some burdens never cease even after we've left the physical world.

Two other volunteers reported to us one day they were arranging displays in the museum. They lifted a small, but hefty, cast iron ice cream store table with two attached stools to move it a few inches. The table was one that was a permanent fixture at the Bass Rutledge Drug Store soda shop during the forties. This would be one of the first places frequented by the cadets of the British Flying Training School. It took both ladies every ounce of their strength to move the table about 10 inches. Suddenly, a loud scraping sound, coming from the second floor, was heard directly over their heads. They described it as if a large, heavy table was being dragged across the entire length of the auditorium upstairs. It was deafening, and they were disturbed because they were confident, they were alone in the building. Startled by what they had just heard, one lady asked if the curator was in his office upstairs and they had simply been unaware of his presence. Both knew this was not the case. In spite, one of the ladies reluctantly climbed the staircase to his office. Just as they had suspected, there was no one upstairs, and the furniture was exactly where it had always been. She could find no explanation for the strange noise.

On another occasion, during a business meeting of the local art association with five people in attendance, there was an unbelievable and unexplained noise event. The downtown area was quiet, it was about 7:00 p.m. on a weeknight. While the members sat around a table in the middle of the first floor, a loud, vibrating, crashing noise seemed to come from the front, South side of the display area. The members were startled to their feet and ran to the exhibit space to see what had happened. They were worried that some of the precious artifacts had surely been destroyed and that one of the large, top-heavy display shelves may have fallen over. To the amazement of all present, there was not a thing out of place. The displays were as precise as they should have been. A couple of the members commented they heard the sound of breaking glass, although some only heard the crash. Looking outside, there was absolutely nothing or anyone around. Although being somewhat rattled, they chalked it up to those Carnegie spirits and continued their business comforted by the fact that others had shared the experience. This was just one of the many reported phantom noises that are commonplace in this beautiful building

One of our Investigators spent several years

volunteering there, helping install displays, opening the doors for Saturday visitors, cleaning, and hosting events. She spent a significant amount of time there and even began to greet the Spirits when she walked into the building. Sometimes that would cause the lights to flicker almost in acknowledgment of her interaction. At least, that is what we like to believe. The place is longstanding, and the wiring is too. In spite, we all are attached to the spirits we think are there. If you are in town, please be sure to say "Hello" from us. They just may flicker the lights for you.

We genuinely hope that some of the city's founders such as "Captain" Robert Terrell and Governor Colquitte enjoy visiting the museum occasionally in the afterlife. The Terrell Heritage Society has done an excellent job of representing the history of Terrell and its founders. If you happen to be in town, we recommend a visit to this museum. Please be sure to sign the guest book when you arrive and let the staff know how you heard about the museum. The Terrell Heritage Society's board members are not convinced there is a haunting of the museum. We respect their thoughts on the matter. At the same time, we do trust the individuals who shared their own experiences with us, and we believe those individuals are convinced they were of a paranormal origin. Many of our team members, myself included, have had firsthand experiences in the building, too. We are convinced there is no organic explanation for those things.

Learn more about the Terrell Heritage Museum by visiting their website at www.terrellheritage.org. They have limited hours, so be sure to check the site before a trip there. The museum is free to attend, but donations are always appreciated and are used to help with the upkeep and restoration of this magnificent building.

THE TERRELL HERITAGE MUSEUM

Our team believes there are many spirits still at the Carnegie Building. Unexplained noises are abundant and a reported shadowman haunts its foyer.

It should be mentioned that the current caretakers of the building disagree with us and do not believe spirits still reside there. They spend a lot of time in the building. We respect their view on the issue but we tell our stories and leave it up to the individual to decide.

6

THE BRITISH FLYING TRAINING SCHOOL

"The popular notion that ghosts are likely to be seen in a graveyard is not borne out by psychical research...A haunting ghost usually haunts a place that a person lived in or frequented while alive... Only a gravedigger's ghost would be likely to haunt a graveyard".

—John Alexander, Ghosts! Washington Revisited: The Ghostlore of the Nation's Capital

THE NO. 1 BRITISH FLYING TRAINING SCHOOL in Terrell was the first training school of its kind. During World War II, RAF flight schools in Europe were being bombed under the hands of the Nazis. The situation was so bleak in 1941 the United States Army Air Corp opened seven training facilities across the United States for young fighter pilots to train without fear of being attacked. Young men came to the United States through Canada, cloaked in darkness, wearing civilian clothing. Most were as young as 18 years old, only children, frightened. They were entering a completely foreign country where everyone was a stranger, and the cultures of their land no longer existed. They could never be sure of their own family's safety back home. Food rationing was severe. Some came malnourished and thin. However, when they arrived and lined up for breakfast that next morning, they found a man standing behind the chow line who asked if they wanted bacon with their eggs. Coming from almost inhumane conditions caused by battle, these young men became brothers, and the next six months were the best time of their lives.

During the week, the cadets trained rigorously, learning incredible maneuvers and feats of skill in small airplanes. When they were not in the air, they spent long hours in the classroom learning the intricate skills of operating aircraft and how to battle their invaders. Those lessons would be challenged when they returned home to fight a dirty war with an uncertain outcome. They began their training in Stearman PT-17's, open cockpit bi-planes, and then they advanced to more sophisticated Harvard AT-6's. The training was stressful and lives, including their own, depended on it. The freedom of their country depended on it. These young men would be heroes.

Out of 2,200 trainees, both instructors and cadets of the School lost a total of 24 lives. Twenty of the lives lost currently lie in a memorial plot dedicated to them in the Oakwood Cemetery on Moore Avenue. The small plot of land holding those graves is recognized as a "little bit of England." Today, men and women from all over the world make the pilgrimage to the city of Terrell to honor these young men every year.

On the weekends the cadets stepped into town and enjoyed dances, parties, Sunday family dinners, and other events hosted by Terrell residents. The Bass-Rutledge Drug Store's Soda Shop was a favorite hangout. Many cadets had rooms in the homes of Terrell residents dedicated solely to them. Members of the community would adopt a soldier every six months just to supply a weekend reprieve from life in the barracks. They met young ladies, made new friends, and had a wonderful time. It was a small escape for those who might die in the war fighting for the freedom of their country. Some of the men who survived the war eventually returned to Terrell after the war, married local women, and adopted the locals as family. Others who didn't survive had written letters to home, and they often spoke about coming back to Terrell when the war was over. I genuinely believe many did come back in spirit. It's hard not to get caught up in the stories of the No 1 British Flying Training School.

Yearly, there are remembrance ceremonies at the cemetery, people will attest they feel the boys standing beside them. Some say they sense eyes being cast upon them during ceremonies as though they are watching themselves being honored for their bravery.

At the site of the school two original hangers still stand, currently being leased by private businesses. Fragments of the airstrip are still identifiable. Recently, the Museum discovered both a Boeing AT-6 and a Stearman PT-17 that were used at the School. The Museum holds many artifacts from the School and photographs of all the classes. One of the largest displays is a map of Texas with Great Britain superimposed over it, with London and Terrell sharing the same point.

I have been told that when conditions are exactly right, you can hear young men's voices and laughter floating on the wind as you stand outside the museum. Directly in front of the museum is the airfield, which was once home to the barracks and the school. If you are fortunate enough to catch this phenomenon, there is no need to be afraid. It is merely the young cadets who left their imprints of joy and camaraderie on the soil, rock, and stone. It is our record player of the past, and it plays on a loop for us to enjoy today. It is the legacy of the young, brave soldiers having the time of their lives left for us so that we do not forget their sacrifice. The boys loved this place, and they loved each other as brothers in the war.

Remembrance ceremonies are held at the cemetery each Memorial and Veterans Day. You can learn more about these events, the museum, and the cadets of the No. 1 British Flying Training School at www.bftsmuseum.org. Visitors are welcome, and donations are highly appreciated. Admission is free

THE CEMETERY PLOT

DEDICATED TO THE BFTS CADETS

Every year the cadets and instructors of the No 1 British Flying Training School who lost their lives in training or at the school are honored. The intensity of the ceremony is such that some claim that they can feel the spirits of the cadets standing by.

7

The Warren Building

"There is no conclusive evidence of any sort of life after death, but there is no evidence against it. Soon enough, you will know, so why fret about it."

—Robert A Heinlein

SENATOR ROBERT WARREN GAVE RISE to this building in or about 1897. Warren practiced law in offices on the second floor while the first floor was home to the Famous Hat Company. Later the ground floor would be occupied by many businesses, including drug stores, furniture stores, and even a gun store. In more recent years, it was given a facelift from a local architectural design expert, Davis Griffith-Cox. Professor Griffith-Cox is a bit of a local celebrity, as he is an eccentric character born and raised in Terrell, along with generations of his family. In future books, we will be sure to talk about Griffith Homeplace Museum and paranormal events we experienced there during our investigations. Those stories would fill an entire book on their own

To make this section of the book easier to categorize, when referring to the Warren Building, we will discuss the original Warren building and the adjacent building. In other words, considering spirits don't see walls then, for the purpose of ease, we don't either.

The Warren Building's façade is as beautiful and intriguing as many of the other storefronts lining Moore Avenue. It has a character of its own and boasts its own unique set of paranormal phenomena. Currently, the two buildings are home to a coffee shop, barber shop, appliance store, boutiques, and residential lofts. It is also zoned for residential, or bed and breakfast status.

Our beloved Lizzie is believed to have been photographed there by occupants of the buildings. Several tour guests have claimed to have captured her apparition in photographs, and others have claimed to have seen her staring out while she stood in an upper floor window of the Warren Building just briefly before disappearing. Although her manifestation is common in the Warren Building, the Anderson Building, found directly across the street has generated enough reports of the young lady it will make your head spin. Her presence is quite common here, and her apparition is often so vivid onlookers first mistake her for a lost little girl instead of the spirit she is. People often speak of other specters they have seen here, and they are just as opaque.

There was once a bakery in the building that had several ghostly encounters of a single spirit that visited the first two weeks the business was open. The employee reporting the story would be in the kitchen. She would hear the door chime and look up to see a woman dressed in Victorian-era clothing, complete with hat and gloves, enter the building. The lady would walk to the couch, sit down, and remove her gloves. Hurriedly, the employee would approach the woman to see if she could help the first customer of the day with a cup of coffee. Yet, as she approached, the woman just suddenly disappeared, leaving no trace of her existence other than this story.

There appears to be a small area between the Anderson building, Old City Hall, and the Warren building where ghosts garner enough energy that they manifest themselves as apparent as you or I. It is highly unusual to have so many similar reports of such solid apparitions in one area. Is there is a ley line or an elevation of electromagnetic energy in this spot, possibly?

Nonetheless, we are happy these ghosts have decided to use it to their own benefit. It certainly makes for a great, if almost unbelievable, story. There is another apparition who tends to appear in this building, and he is affectionately referred to as the cowboy. He had been seen so clearly and so often that one witness was able to identify him in a photograph taken circa 1930 when the building was the Famous Hat Company. We stumbled upon several pictures shared via social media during the restoration of the Warren building. As so often occurs in these old buildings, there are usually several changes that need to happen before a place can be open to the public. This was the case on the second floor of the building. I mention this because we can assure there was no contamination by anyone but those working in that space. However, the sawdust left to settle on the floor the night before had been strangely imprinted by cowboy boots.

As is often the case, renovations in old buildings appear to generate higher reports of potential paranormal activity. Our research uncovered a recent story about the strange misplacement of blue painters' tape that was being used to mark the walls for remodeling. Mysteriously, sometime during the night, the tape had been removed from the carefully measured areas and replaced randomly in obscure places. Workers would arrive to find blue tape placed on the staircase, windows, floors, and other bizarre areas where it was not needed. This resulted in the requirement of exact replacement of the tape in preparation for painting.

The Warren building is adjacent to residential lofts, and some renters have recounted their own stories to us. It is common for disembodied voices to be heard, whistling, and other mysterious sounds made by someone unseen. One resident couple reported a large painting hanging above their bed was removed from its place on the wall and found, the next morning, on the floor leaning against the opposite wall. Another resident expressed concern because she often finds her two-year-old sitting in front of the bedroom closet while babbling "toddler-speak" for great lengths of time as if someone invisible was entertaining him. To make matters stranger, the resident states that the child's eyes follow some unseen object around the room. Either one of these behaviors would be considered eerie by themselves, but to make things more bizarre are the sudden, intense cold spots that suddenly appear in the same area by the child's mother.

ORIGINAL WARREN BUILDING

(*Addition Not Shown In Photo*)

The Warren building and its addition are rumored to be one of the places Lizzie has been seen and photographed. It is also said that a cowboy hangs out there.

8

The Train Depot

"Railroad Iron is a magician's rod, in its power to evoke the sleeping energies of land and water."

—Ralph Waldo Emerson

ONE DAY A CALL CAME INTO THE OFFICE asking if we could come down to the old Texas & Pacific Railroad freight depot to set up a time to speak to a local community group. Walking in the door, we were instantly swarmed by a group of friendly, and excited staff, that could not wait to share their own personal stories about the place. For a haunted tour guide operator, this place was an absolute dream! The old freight depot was built in 1911 and operated as a depot until 1977. It has been converted into a beautiful set of office spaces, but most of the original structure remained to keep to the unique context of the building. This is undoubtedly the most beautifully restored historical building in Terrell, Texas. It is a real mixture of contemporary meets the historical past in one building. That historical past not only included the property but, according to the employees officed in this building, also continued to be the home of a ghostly figure they affectionately called, "The Conductor."

Paranormal investigators discuss two primary kinds of hauntings: Intelligent hauntings and residual hauntings. Residual hauntings are those that seem to play along on a loop as if a recording were repeatedly playing. When periods of high emotional energy are present, that energy is believed to imprint itself into the organic structures of the area, including the soil, trees, stone, and more. These areas are most notorious for the negative or darker incidents such as accidents, violent crimes, or horrific scenes of war. However, the same theory holds true for positive experiences such as where the boys of the British Flying Training School stayed during their time here in the U.S. This is reported as the sounds of the boy's laughter and voices carrying across the fields and into the wind. This is to be heard by those who happen to be in the right place, at the right time, and during the right conditions. Those that experience a residual haunting should consider themselves fortunate as a living person rarely observes them. Based on the information we have received from the witnesses at the old Freight Depot, I am confident that this is a residual haunting. It is a perfect example of an energetic tape loop reminding us all about the professionals who proudly spent their lives working for the railroad.

Two ladies shared the office in front of the depot. They spoke to us about an evening when they were both working late due to a project deadline. Out of nowhere, they heard footsteps, walking at first and then moving into a fast run or jog. Both ladies were startled but made their way to the long wooden hallway that divided the building into offices on the right and on the left. They saw absolutely nothing but what they heard sent shivers up their spines. As they both stood and looked down the hallway, there was the clear sound of footsteps starting at the most distal part of the building, followed (in sound only) by a quick increase in speed as the noise ran towards them.

I understand this train depot once received and shipped freight. Expensive parcels needed to be held in a secured area. As a result, the building had a small space, secured with grated bars, preventing access to anyone without a key. Parcels would be placed here, processed, then shipped when the time was right, all the while, protected under the watchful eye of the station master. These parcel cages are still intact in the building.

This was never illustrated better than the story shared with me by one employee. She stated she casually walked towards the front portion of the depot only to be surprised by a man, dressed in overalls and a typical conductor's hat. He appeared to be making motions as if stamping then writing on something. We speculate, was an unseen logbook. Standing in the secured, grated area, the Conductor's apparition paid absolutely no mind to the employee that stepped in on him. This behavior is one clue that leads paranormal investigators to classify this as a residual haunting. The specter seemed to be performing a task that he may have conducted during his job, and his lack of interaction with the employee tells us that she had seen an energetic imprint.

One gentleman claimed he watched the "Conductor" walk directly through a wall into the gentlemen's restroom. Of course, there is no longer any type of door there, so the apparition simply made the same type of movements he would have made when he was living. This is another hallmark of a residual haunting. Spirits just go through the motions they did earlier with disregard to any structural changes to the building or space.

More stories on the old Freight Depot are out there, but there wasn't enough time that day to hear about them all. We hope to go back soon and take more time to visit with the tenants there. This fantastic, little building must hold a million secrets in its walls.

THE TRAIN DEPOT

The employees at the renovated Train Depot speak fondly of the ghostly "Conductor" who continues his duties. He has been spotted inside one of the secured, grated areas performing tasks he once did when he worked there. His footsteeps can sometimes be heard walking down the long corridor that lies in between the new offices.

9

THE BRIN BUILDING

"There are an infinite number of universes existing side by side and through which our consciousnesses constantly pass. In these universes, all possibilities exist. You are alive in some, long dead in others, and never existed in still others. Many of our 'ghosts' could indeed be visions of people going about their business in a parallel universe or another time – or both."

—Paul F. Eno
Faces at the Window

FOR THE SIMPLE EASE OF CATEGORIZING our buildings we have included the real estate located on Moore Avenue between Catherine and Adelaide Street "The Brin

Building." The entire block was not owned by Terrell's prominent Brin family, but they did own the most famous section of the building. This section would be most known as the Brin Opera House. The entire building had been home to billiards halls, saloons, barber shops and more. Since it was built in the late 1800s the whole section had taken many forms. We occupied the building next door to the former Brin Opera House for several years, and it was never a dull moment.

Our location held a piece of the Brin's operations in the form of a gigantic safe. The ancient object safely secured the personal goods and money used for business affairs. As temporary caretakers of the Brin safe, we had many opportunities for a variety of mediums to "read" the safe and its alleged secrets. The enormous metal multi-doored box dated back to 1855 and weighed in at a whopping 2-3 tons. One could assume the sheer size and the materials of its construct contributed to an enormous amount of energy that was palpable by even the least sensitive people. No doubt, it was an ideal trigger object, and we would gather our guests around it for short examples of investigation techniques. They would 'ooh,' and 'ahh' as the lights and noises from the proximity meters would flash in response to their questions. Every paranormal investigator will tell you having an object of this magnitude, you should expect a spirit or two to come with it. Those working in the office would agree that perhaps, Mr. and Mrs. Brin weren't so ready to let go of that safe.

Our investigations taught us that Mr. Brin was not fond of women touching the safe. It was a common belief at the time that the patriarch in the household was to manage the money, and the women took care of the "softer" family needs. This attitude may have been in the atmosphere, but the spirit of Mrs. Brin was not a quiet one. Evidence, in many forms, seemed to indicate she was an integral part of whatever business that safe was associated with. There are so many details told about the object it would require another book altogether.

The Brin safe dates to 1855 and weighs at least 2 tons. It has survived at least one fire and has secrets that we will never know about. Before our offices moved into the building, there was a businessman in the location. This man was an integral part in helping us get started in Terrell, and we wanted to return the kindness by providing exposure for him. The issue was that there weren't any real ghost stories that we could tell about his building. However, there was a minor incident. It wasn't a great ghost story and could likely be explained, but we used it to our advantage to promote his business space.

On a couple occasions, the agent entered his building in the mornings to find that both bathroom sink faucets, even the non-working hot water faucet, were standing wide open and water was running full blast. Of course, the plumbing in these buildings was ancient, so we assumed it was the probable cause of the issue. Our tour guide would take the group by the business and mention the faucet incidents, leaving them to make up their own minds. It was a brief way to get his business noticed without taking time from our other, more-enticing stories. About two years later, we moved directly behind his business, with only a conference room serving as a buffer between his agency and our headquarters. It was at that time we inadvertently stirred up more spirit activity than we could have ever hoped for.

Caution: Area May Have Moving Objects

Objects simply started moving on their own and in the most unusual ways. More than once, I would be sitting at my computer, engaged in a project, when half the contents of my desk would simply fall off onto the floor. It was as if someone took their forearm and swept everything off in one quick motion. Paperwork, stapler, computer mouse, cell phone, and any other item occupying my workspace just slipped off onto the floor in one swift action. This elicited a joyful laugh every time because it was as though someone, I could not see was trying to garner my attention. On other occasions, the first person to arrive in the morning would find my stack of reference books, carefully housed with bookends on the window sill the night before, scattered all over the office floor, far away from where they sat the night before. Initially, we scratched our heads, but it soon became apparent, as ghostly activity became more evident, we were dealing with a joking spirit.

The movement of objects started to become routine, but I can recall one strange day being floored by the sheer force the spirits could use to throw an object. Earlier that day, a fellow investigator was standing by the sink, and he noticed a tube of lip balm. He alerted me to its presence since I was always searching for my lip balm and could never find it. He placed the container by the sink, which was about 12-feet from my workspace. The moment was quickly forgotten until later that afternoon when I turned away from my desk and turned back in time to see the last foot in the flying trajectory of that tube of lip balm. When it hit the cabinet behind me, it created a loud bang, and the sheer force of the power behind it caused the magnetic-clasped cabinet door to open about an inch. The other investigator jumped at the noise. After a short episode of laughter, I apologized to the spirit who threw it. He or she was feeling a bit ignored. This was an effective tactic to get our attention as we spent the rest of the day, knowing we were not alone in our day-to-day bustle. Did I mention this was an incredible place to work? Surely most business offices didn't include invisible co-workers in their decision making.

Our favorite spirits in the building were never shy around an audience. Others were often around to report what were inexplicable events which always helped our claims. One late afternoon, the team was working one of Terrell's small business events. The day had been a busy one with large numbers of shoppers in the area and team members scattered around the two offices helping guests and answering questions. The doors had been propped open all day long, enjoying the beautiful weather. Sitting in the center of the office with a guest and her granddaughter when we started to notice something bizarre. Three of us sat watching this door slowly moving on its own. It shifted slowly enough that the guest and I had at least three opportunities to turn our attention to each other then back to the door. The door slowly closed to about one foot from its threshold, and then it slammed shut with such an alarming force it rattled the photos on the wall. The doors had been open all day and had not moved an inch, and it was clear there was another force at work. The atmosphere during the incident seemed different. It is difficult to put into words, but I would equate the feeling to what you would sense in the moments before a Texas tornado, something most of us Southerners know entirely too well. There was an unnerving stillness to the air that was nothing short of eerie.

Now I See You, Now I Don't: The Apparitions

Several days later, another investigator at the event told us about his encounter that happened minutes before we saw the door slam. He had an actual spirit encounter. It happened in the room next to us. He had propped a swinging door open with a small, empty trashcan. The door, that was too heavy to be secured by this flimsy object, repeatedly swung closed. As he was looking for something to secure the door properly, the door swung closed again. During one of these moments, the door swung outward, the investigator noticed a woman who had wandered into the small break area next to the room. This space was simply a small break area and he at once became perplexed by her movements toward an interior wall. Thinking she must be lost or getting a cup of coffee from the small coffeemaker in the area, he went to welcome her. For just a second he got a quick, unobstructed view of the form. He described her clothing as being solid black, "gauze-like," and flowing but unable to say if it was a blouse or a dress. He was observant enough to see she was dressed professionally. At that moment, he assumed she was a guest, and she just stepped in quietly. Politely he said, "Hello ma'am. I'll be right with you." and as he stepped forward into the small area, the well-dressed woman had vanished into thin air, as if she walked through the interior wall. The only other witness did not see the apparition but did hear the investigator speak to the woman as though she was a customer.

Before moving our headquarters into this space, it had been used as a storage area. The Brin safe had not been touched in years and was used as a space for mounds of paperwork. It was a mess. The busy office up front took precedence over cleaning in this back room. We set about the task of cleaning this fantastic treasure trove of items that had not been touched in years. Not surprisingly, our busy cleaning stirred up the spiritual energy that had been quietly settled for a long time.

Our intuition was right. As we were leaving

through the front door, I turned in time to see a white orb, greater than the size of the door threshold itself move from right to left in the room we had just worked in. The ball was misty and fog-like in nature. The excitement was overwhelming because there were almost no reported experiences of anything paranormal in the building before. Suddenly, here is this enormous paranormal slap in the face as I watched the ghostly orb moving in the room. Calling out to my teammate, I wanted to confirm he had laid his own eyes on the orb. Unfortunately, I was the only witness.

The last apparition I witnessed there I was completely startled. Never fearful of the energies present in the building, it was completely unexpected. Left with excitement and exhilaration that was challenging to define, I was utterly shaken. Nursing a bad back and needing to be in the office so early the next day I decided to get some shut eye on the air mattress for the night. The goal was to be fresh for the next day instead of making the pilgrimage home. Sitting on the air mattress low off the floor there was enough ambient light from the conference room and the television, I clearly saw the tall figure of a man's shadowy silhouette. The shadow ghost stepped about six feet to my right, and I laid my central vision directly on the specter. Where I was sitting, he was slightly taller than the average man. It was difficult to tell since I was practically sitting on the floor myself. There were no features on his face or body nor clothes to identify. It was merely a shadow. It was not like stories I have heard by others, where they experience a sense of doom and evil with the appearance of a "shadow person." In fact, I felt protected, looked over. Other women working in the building have expressed the same sense. It was as if our specter was protective of us and wanted to ensure we never felt alone.

The shadow figure's head seemed elongated and only partially manifested and was still trying to appear. His arms seemed to be long and thin. His head aside, he was just the shape of an average person. I sent a text to our Office Manager, so I had immediate record of what I experienced. Typing in the text message, I was shaking so badly I could not manage my fingers on the small, electronic keyboard. Switching to the voice to text feature on my cell phone, I realized that my voice was equally as shaky and came out like a small child's voice. Now, I laugh at how shaken I had allowed myself to get. It was from pure excitement as I had never had such a close encounter.

The Departed Have a Sense of Humor Too

One sunny day, my husband, my son, and I went in to clean the office. I had just purchased a new sundress and was feeling particularly pretty in it. At the sink washing my hands, one of the boys grabbed the back of my dress and started to pull on it with enough force, I took a step to balance myself from falling. Turning to tell them to leave it alone, I realized that no one was behind me. Maybe, Mrs. Brin or another female occupant was telling me that she approved of my new ensemble? Mrs. Brin was considered one of the elites in Terrell and a nod to my dress would be regarded as a compliment.

By this point, the phenomenon about the bathroom faucets were forgotten. Going on about our business, satisfied with the encounters everyone had experienced was enough for us to believe the place was haunted. It was two years in the building before the ghosts began to play tricks with the faucets again. Once it started, it became a regular thing. The bathroom faucets started turning themselves on when no one was near the sink. An agent, new to the office was alone working at her desk when she suddenly heard water running. She was embarrassed to say anything initially, but several days later, she had worked up the courage to mention it to me.

The experience seemed to be of ghostly origin to her, but she didn't want to jump to any conclusions and initially felt a little silly about the whole thing. She had never heard the story before and was glad to know that she had some validation, and that she was not alone in her experience. It was just several days before her account the regular agent had come into our office to ask if one of us had left the sink running as it came on while he was working up front. Of course, no one had. This phenomenon soon became regarded as a typical event for us.

The spirits enjoyed playing pranks on all of us during the time we were most vulnerable. That is to say that the bathroom became a source of nervousness for all of us. The bathroom door would shake and rattle as if someone were at the door. Other times, the simple hook lock would just pop off the eye hook that it was seated in as you were taking a tinkle.

One evening, the agent told me he had locked everything up for the night. About two hours after he left, and the sun had gone down for the day, I excused myself to go to the bathroom. Alone in the building, I did not bother to lock the bathroom door. The distinct sound of someone entering the building through the front door was heard. An old-fashioned bell was hanging over the door so that we could hear someone coming in if we were in the back. Reaching up quietly as possible, I locked the bathroom door. Being unarmed and in a vulnerable position, I sat quietly looking for something to fight with if necessary. Armed with nothing but a sad and shameful bottle of mouthwash, I listened for footsteps or shuffling from an intruder. Hearing nothing moving about the building, I finally stepped out of the bathroom and using my biggest "bad dog" voice I called out to the room, demanding someone answer me and announcing I was armed. I had this lethal bottle of mouthwash to protect myself, but they didn't need to know that, right? Feeling comfortable that I was alone, I walked to the front door, finding it locked and secured. After that, we heard the door open and often close with the distinct sound of the tinkling bell. Eventually, we listened to the mystery bell so often we simply began to ignore it as it was becoming a repeated distraction.

We miss working in that building. We will miss the spirits there. Our experiences there will not soon be forgotten. Alas, new opportunities await the living, and the living must pursue them!

10

Terrell State Hospital

"Perfer et obdura, dolor hic tibi proderit olim."

(Translated: Be patient and tough; someday this pain will be useful to you.)

ONE WOULD BE REMISS IF THERE were not a section dedicated to the most controversial and spoken about alleged haunted spot in the city: The Terrell State Hospital. The hospital is a state-owned and managed facility used for the acute treatment of those struggling with varying degrees of psychiatric illness. Most Terrell residents (and those in local area towns) have heard at least one story about an unusual happening. There is no shortage of people eager to share a story, including the local police officers who stopped us during the tour regularly just to tell us about a recent call, usually a probable trespasser. Verbal accounts and the occasional email reach us regularly. Large numbers of stories are handed down by former employees and, at times, a rare temporary resident. The talk of ghostly apparitions and unexplained phenomenon have been occurring since it began operation in the late 1800s when it was still referred to as the North Texas Lunatic Asylum.

These accounts are reported to have occurred over the entire area of the hospital's grounds, which cover over 600 acres of land. Initially, the hospital was self-sustaining, with dairy and farming. Terrell State Hospital includes a newer, contemporary, and functioning facility. There is a significant amount of grounds where there are dilapidated buildings that were formally part of the functioning hospital. It also is home to its own, "Wildwood Cemetery," at the very back of the property, and homes that were once occupied by the Superintendent and other administrative staff. Today, the hospital grounds are accessible from one gate at the East end of Brin Street. A security guard is aware of cars entering and leaving, and a security guard or two drive the grounds. Although this is a state-owned, publicly funded facility, health-care privacy laws restrict some general activity, including photography. Paranormal investigative groups will not be welcomed, so don't even think about that.

Fascination, and unnecessary taboo, with mental illness, automatically conjure up images of people who have problems that seem, to the uneducated, as frightening, and scary. Buying into media and movie propaganda, the oblivious automatically conjure up images of people performing unnatural acts of screaming in straitjackets or speaking in tongues. These false stories are further fed by barbaric and equally terrifying inhumane treatments. Mental illness rarely manifests with such intensity. Fortunately, with a far better understanding of the human brain, the treatments used today are in the form of much more successful medications and therapy. Even though medicine has made tremendous advances in the treatment and management of such diseases, it never fails, when we take these long-held, erroneous misconceptions and combine it with a ghost story, two subjects most people do not understand, it creates the perfect storm for enigmatic misunderstanding and intense curiosity.

There are thousands of stories held in the walls of the hospital formerly known as the "North Texas Lunatic Asylum." No one can say there are not cases of extreme suffering in dire need of help that is not helped with a pill or injection, but these are the rarity. However, they are not locked away to be forgotten.

There are rumors many moons ago a handful of perfectly sane wives were admitted by hateful husbands claiming stories of hysteria. The actual truth is the men simply grew tired of their spouses and either decided to live out their days as bachelors or with their younger mistresses. Personally, I shudder to think that if I had been born in a different era, I might have been committed to the hospital, myself, about fifty pounds and many gray hairs ago.

Once every couple of months the tour would be stopped by a Terrell police officer hoping to share a recent call about someone reported on the unused grounds. Terrell's PD is the epitome of a fantastic police force. They are in great physical shape, well-trained, and armed. In spite, most are not embarrassed to admit these reports make them nervous. According to the officers that have reported the stories to us, they say they will not exit their vehicles when called to the unused part of the grounds at night unless necessary. They offer no shame or embarrassment about this. Mostly, the calls are about a woman who is repeatedly seen in one dilapidated building centered in the middle of the grounds. The rumor is that this structure was once used to hold the patients that no one could control. We do know that this practice did exist in other similar institutions across the United States. If this did occur at Terrell State Hospital, we land on the side of oblivion. Even still, the report of the woman is still consistent from multiple, reliable sources with close ties to the hospital, the police officers included.

Emails come to us often from a variety of people reporting they have seen shadows roaming the halls of the treatment wards. The departed here do not seem to mind the new roomies endlessly rotated in and out of the buildings for treatment. They continue to live in the afterlife doing their afterlife things, so-to-speak. These were residual hauntings of patients or staff merely going about things in their earlier lives like an endless loop of recorded energy. Some emails did not even describe specific events. They simply wanted to drive home the point that the hospital was very, very haunted with no desire to leave any further details.

At one time, firefighters and EMT's used the abandoned buildings to conduct regular training. One fireman described a mannequin they used for practice so heavy it took two physically fit firemen to lift it. To carry it up and down the stairs was a huge and painstaking undertaking. The weight of the mannequin offered an opportunity for the men and women to practice the realistic evacuation of a victim. During several days of training, they arrived one morning to find the mannequin missing from its original place on the first floor. The firefighter relaying the story to us remembered how odd it was because the day prior, they all had a detailed discussion about how they were leaving it there. No one wanted to move it merely due to the manpower needed to move it upstairs.

The only reason they pondered moving it was the highly unlikely event that someone would want to steal it. After they considered there was a secured gate, a locked door, it was of no monetary value, and it would take an act of God to move, they decided to leave it. They had joked about it so much that it was cemented in everyone's mind exactly where they left it. Imagine the surprise when they found the missing mannequin on the second floor. At least two strong men were needed to move the body but not a man fessed up to the event, and only one person held the key to the building. If it had been a joke, it would have been hard to keep secret. If it were paranormal, it would have had to have been one strong spirit to move that object to the second floor. How do you explain it? If you can figure it out, then I know a group of young, strong, perplexed firemen who want to know.

One of the stories that we occasionally come across is that of a woman in white. She is reported to be visible in one of the dilapidated buildings in the center of the abandoned property through a window. We took two mediums by that building on separate occasions. Neither medium knew each other nor had ever met. Both reported, not knowing our stories, that there is a woman there. Why this spirit would be there is something we do not know nor can speculate on. Curiously, the trees that are growing on all sides of this building are growing outward and away from the building. I've sent this to several gardeners and they mention that the trees may be reaching towards the sun or that years of the wind blowing through those areas may have caused the trees to change growth trajectory. This is reasonable, of course, except we find it strange that it happens around the entire building. Simply something to ponder about.

We honor the privacy of the staff and patients at the Terrell State Hospital. We tell ghost stories associated with the facility but in no manner do we intend to imply disrespect.

A part of the proceeds of this book is dedicated to the Terrell State Hospital. Be sure to follow us on social media for potential fundraising events aimed to help the

Terrell State Hospital's Patient Volunteer Services, which supplies personal items such as clothing and toiletries for the patients. Many such things are not provided by state funds.

ABANDONED BUILDING AT TERRELL STATE HOSPITAL

This is the location where a mysterious woman in white has been reported.

11

THE ANDERSON BUILDING

"Death is not the end, it is simply walking out of the physical form and into the spirit realm, which is our true home. It's going back home... We unzip the body, so-to-speak let it fall to the ground and walk through the next door clothed in our spiritual form, which was always there inside the physical body."

---Lianne Willowmoon
Soul Antiquary

THE ANDERSON BUILDING IS A MAMMOTH of a structure. It is on the Northeast corner of East Moore Avenue and Adelaide Street. The residents in Terrell refer to it as the "White's Building" because it previously held the White's dry goods store. Our team calls it the Anderson Building because that is clearly engraved on the top of the building, eluding to the fact that someone with the surname "Anderson" was the original builder of the structure itself. The five-floor construct has a full underground basement (which we count as a floor), and when compared to the other businesses on Moore Avenue, it stands alone in size. As of this writing, the only operational levels are the basement and the first and second floors. The basement, I have been told, was once used for dry goods storage. It holds two small rooms and has drains in the concrete floor. It also has a rear metal exterior door that slides up and down with a descending concrete slide that allows the accessible entrance of materials into the basement. The entire structure makes it an ideal space for storing dry goods. Ironically, it is rumored to have been a morgue in later years when the second and third floors became home to a small privately-owned hospital. Considering the design of the basement, it would have made for an equally efficient morgue. Residents who lived in Terrell their entire lives swear it was never used for such purposes; however, we have heard a substantial number of stories to the contrary. So many stories, that we simply cannot dismiss the fact that this could be a genuine possibility. Having been in the basement, personally, on more than one occasion, I believe that it would have served that purpose at one time. No matter how morbid this may be, every city must have such a service. Considering this was a hospital for decades, it seems very reasonable these could be more than rumors.

The last time I was in the building's basement, it had punching bags hanging the entire length of the ample space. Like most basements, the area is as you expect: dark, damp, musty, and cold. The first floor, level with East Moore Avenue, is a fitness gym equipped with workout equipment, including free weights and machines. The second floor is an extension of the fitness gym reserved to classes including boxing, martial arts, among others. It also houses tanning beds and shower rooms. Numerous guests on the ghost tour attested to uncomfortable experiences while they were members of the gym. They shared stories of being pinched or touched, having their hair pulled or stroked while using the gym equipment by some unseen frisky hand. Overall, they all agreed it was just plain creepy there.

The third and fourth floors have incredible views of East Moore Avenue. There are no utilities on these floors, so building code does not allow their use. The spaces are in disarray with broken windows, construction material, and dead birds strewn about. Apparent medical books still line shelves, and there are tiny rooms with glass windows looking into them, reminiscent of infant nurseries. With a little work and love, those top floors could be home to beautiful offices or a great Bed and Breakfast. As often is the case with these older buildings, the expense of bringing these floors up to city code would be so costly that it is not practical to do so. It is a real shame that such a historic landmark has levels that lie in shambles.

SPIRITUAL YIN AND YANG...

Our team spent four short days there renovating a space on the second floor of the Anderson building before a rental agreement snafu was discovered. Although we hated to leave, the best thing for all parties was to move on. We were grateful for getting to spend time working side-by-side with its ghosts, even if we were not aware of their immediate presence. It is impossible to explain the intensity of the atmosphere there. Being on any one of its five floors brings on feelings that are powerful and exciting. The air is palpable. It possesses a different mix of staleness and electrical charge. One area may bring on a less than pleasant sensation, and others are overwhelmingly positive. It is almost as if there is a battle of each power, keeping both in a constant balance. The positive cancels out the negative and vice versa.

LOOK TWICE

The building just next to the Anderson boasts accounts of apparitions so solidly manifested they look as real as you or I. Spirits reported are described with such clarity they are mistaken to be customers and approached by helpful staff. The employee would inquire to the customer as to how they may help them only to suddenly become stunned as the apparition would vaporize right before their eyes. This triangle between the Anderson and Warren buildings and Old City Hall, immediately behind the Warren building on Adelaide Street, are unusually active areas for reasons we cannot explain. Witnesses tell stories of many specters in these buildings. One is a young girl we have named "Lizzie."

SHE NEEDED A NAME...

The young girl mentioned above is reported to be seen in businesses up and down Moore Avenue, even being seen walking the sidewalks. Most accounts seem to occur at the Anderson building. Described to be around eight or nine years old with long hair and a white dress donning a black sash around her waist, she manifests with exceptional clarity.

The little girl was mentioned on our tour so often that we needed something to call her. Being of such a young age, it only seemed appropriate to provide her with an identity. "The team eventually landed on the name "Lizzie" based on multiple impressions shared with us by numerous mediums. Psychic Medium Steph, a well-respected medium who is also talented in remote viewing, identifies her birth name as "Elizabeth" and even believes she is buried in a cemetery southeast of Terrell. Although we conducted research to identify this child, we were unable to do so. There was a theory she is the daughter of Senator Robert Warren. However, that was dispelled. The sheer abundance of her reported sightings provided us an obligation to give her a name.

One of our tour guests captured a photograph of

what appeared to be a young girl peering from a window of the Warren building. Another guest had a similar photo of what might have been an apparition of Lizzie, too. The guests allowed me to share the pictures with the lady who owned the Anderson at that time. She was someone who believed she had seen Lizzie on multiple occasions. Immediately she pointed at the first photo and said, "This is her. I would recognize her anywhere." The photograph showed what appeared to be a short form, with a white dress and a black sash around the waist. What convinced me was the absolute confidence in the owner's voice when she saw it. At least in her mind, there was no doubt.

A gym employee brought her little girl to work one day. Her daughter was around 11-years old and had been at the building very often without incident. During that visit, however, the daughter claimed to witness Lizzie coming into a room and trying to physically turn the doorknob into another room. The little girl did not mention the incident to her mother. Instead, she started to refuse to return to the gym and became insistent, if not downright fitful, that she stay home by herself. She absolutely refused to go to the gym without having a crying episode, which was unlike the child. The concerned mother pried harder, wanting to know why this strange behavior began so suddenly. Previously, the little girl loved to go to work with her as she enjoyed playing on the many floors offering unique opportunities for a child's active imagination. Incessant amounts of prodding resulted in her daughter detailing an account with Lizzie's apparition. Most adults would be frightened by seeing a ghost, so understandably her daughter, was scared and never wanted to step foot in the building again

Dancing Orbs

On occasion, while standing across the street from the Anderson, myself, and others have awed at dancing light orbs in the building. During one ghost tour, the tour guide and guests sat down on the tall stepped curb and watched for all of ten minutes while the lights blinked and danced. Sometimes the illumination would appear in the window of a room which we knew to be locked and closed off from the remainder of the floor. The repeating rows of windows give excellent visual access to each floor. These orbs are always seen on the third floor, where there is no electricity. These strange small circular balls are illuminated red, and they almost appear to be enjoying themselves darting around in unusual patterns. It was easy to rule out organic reasons for such brilliance, such as the reflection of cars, traffic lights, or someone in the building with a flashlight.

One employee shared her experience in the gym at the Anderson. Just after cleaning off one of the weight machines, she walked back to her desk to sit down at her chair. Suddenly, a small, green-colored orb elevated from the machine and flew across the room, back again, returning to the same machine she had just cleaned. It proceeded to hover in a manner that the witness felt as though the orb wanted to be acknowledged in some way. She watched the spherical object for what seemed like an eternity. As an attempt to stop the frightening experience, she spoke up and said shakily, "I know that you're here, but you are frightening me." The green orb disappeared. She told us she was confident the ball of light was a manifestation of her husband trying to reconnect. He had passed a year earlier, and he was a frequent, almost daily attendee at the gym.

THE ANDERSON BUILDING

This is where we witnessed strange orbs navigating from one floor to another (top two floors). At the time, there was no electricity on those levels.

One Fateful Fall Brings a Difficult Decision

So, I was having one of those days. You know the kind I'm talking about. The type of days where you think the world is punishing you for some sort of karmic displeasure you put into the universe when you were a teenager. Leaving a doctor's visit, I had an issue with a prognosis that would affect my ability to focus on my business. I wasn't sure if I was going to manage. I loved what I did. The paranormal was more than just entertainment to me. I saw how it impacted people's lives, and I was glad to be part of a team that provided a service to help when people didn't have anywhere else to go. We never charged for investigations, and we did a lot of free work, but we managed to find legitimate, honest ways to make a profit with our work. That allowed us to do the things we loved to do and help people feel accepted and safe.

Well, I stepped into the elevator to have an encounter with a beautiful, middle-aged black woman. Pleasantries were exchanged, and it was not anything that seemed out of the ordinary in any way, but it felt different in a way. "How are you today?" I asked. Her response, "I am blessed," indicating to me that she was a God-fearing woman. She asked about me, and I responded that despite it all I honestly couldn't complain about a thing. I was blessed too.

At that time, I had been struggling with health, additional weight from medications, and extreme pain in my foot. My doctor sent me to have an MRI across the street, and I got lost. Finding my compass, I rushed into the crosswalk, but my movements were like a drunk giraffe in stilettos. I fell in the crosswalk and couldn't get to my feet. Cars lined up, passengers staring at their phones, and no one person made any motion to help me get to my feet. I was humiliated and disgusted. I decided at that very moment that I would close my office doors forever. After all, who would miss us? Ego bruised but myself uninjured, I managed to my feet. Cane in hand, I turned to the line of cars and gave my best curtsy to the offending traffic. Admittedly, I don't have to explain the dirty words I was calling those people in my mind.

Arriving at the imaging center, I stood at the front door and broke down in tears. My mind was made up, I was closing the business.

ENTER THE ANGEL

Taking a seat in the lobby this sweet, almost angelic voice speaks up from behind me. The voice said, "Had I known that you were coming here, then we could have walked together." Turning to see the source of the voice it was the lady from the elevator. This chance meeting turned into an hour-long conversation that would change everything.

She asked me what I did, and I told her about the ghost tours and our investigation team located in Terrell. She says to me that she grew up there. I love Terrell. However, she had a very different view of the city.

During the height of segregation, she had grown up "on the wrong side of the tracks." It was a dark time in history, and few discuss it today. We had uncovered historical information about extreme racism in Kaufman County while researching investigations in the area. On one investigation, our medium had impressions of white men lined up, walking across fields, looking for freed black men, women and, children who would be sold back into slavery. This was a program instituted by the state government in 1846, dubbed "Slave Patrols." This was not isolated to Terrell or Kaufman County but occurred all over the South. Even though Mary, my new friend, was not old enough to experience that fear she had experienced the racism that continued long after. She had no fear to speak about things that are kept hidden today. She spoke of the hurt, the isolation, and how the color of her skin caused tension and turmoil. Her story required me to stifle back tears. I received an education, first-hand, that day, and I will always be grateful for her honesty.

Still processing the information I had just heard, I almost didn't realize when she started to speak of Dr. Fridel, the physician, who operated his hospital on the first and second floors of the Anderson building. Dr. Fridel only treated white patients, as was the standard then, but he was well loved by everyone. Dr. Fridel had a nurse who was a black woman, and it is reported she had been with him for 20 years. My new friend told me the following story: Dr. Fridel's nurse found it challenging to have a child. Eventually, she managed to give birth to two beautiful children. Both babies were delivered by Dr. Fridel. Sadly, a few days after the birth of her second child, she developed complications. Dr. Fridel took every possible measure to save her life. After she crossed over, the kind doctor held her hand for an hour and a half, before the staff convinced him to call time of death. Dr.

Fridel had deeply loved his professional partner and friend. I can only imagine the immense pain he suffered at this loss.

DOES THE NURSE STILL RESIDE IN ANDERSON?

Several weeks after this intense encounter with the stranger on the elevator, my breath was taken away when a woman posted on Facebook that while waiting at the traffic light intersecting East Moore Avenue and Adelaide Street, she happened to glance up at the side of the Anderson building. In the window, she witnessed a black woman, dressed in an old-fashioned nurses' uniform, complete with the starched white hat sitting atop her head, crossing behind the windows on the second floor. She reported that she couldn't believe her eyes and instantly knew she saw an apparition. She called her sister to tell her what she had witnessed and inquired what the building had been in the past. Previous to her posting on Facebook, she had no knowledge the structure had been home to Dr. Fridel's hospital several decades earlier. She certainly had no experience of Dr. Fridel and his beloved nurse. I was exhilarated there was finally confirmation of this beautiful, albeit tragic story.

As for the angel I met that day, I had asked her to call me, and we would have lunch together. I told her we would walk up and down the shops of Moore Avenue and shop together as friends. Two years later, I'm still waiting for her phone call. I wonder if she will ever know the impact she had on my life and if I will ever have a chance to share the amazing story of the nurse's apparition in the window of the Anderson building, as she seemingly continued her work.

Another intriguing story this woman shared with me was about her own personal struggles, living with the burden of being a clairvoyant. She would often have dreams of tragedies that would come to fruition days later. One of these misfortunes involved the drowning of a child which deeply disturbed her because she was unable to change the circumstances of the event. She had no idea how to deal with this burden (or gift, depending upon how you view it). Since our business works to help people just like her, I had confirmation I was exactly where I needed to be. I was tremendously grateful God saw to place this Angel in front of me.

A Visit from Lizzie?

This chapter would not be complete without me sharing my own personal story of the Anderson. The short time we spent in the building, we had started a full renovation project. The project began with restoring the original floors that lay beneath the worn linoleum flooring in a large, windowed room on the Northwest corner of the building. One day, my team and I were sweeping and running the shop vacuum to pick up all the dust. Out of nowhere, I felt a powerful and fantastic presence with me. Earlier in the day, we had conducted an electronic voice session using our investigative equipment to let the spirits know we were there for them. We went on to let them know it was okay to make themselves known and we wouldn't be frightened by any activity they might elect to show us. We had hoped this would increase the paranormal activity, but when this sudden presence stumbled upon me, I was taken entirely by surprise. The hair stood up on my arms and the back of my neck. My fellow Investigator and I looked at each other with wide eyes. Both of us had felt the same thing. Was it the young lady Lizzie, we had so often told stories about? Perhaps, it was Dr. Fridel's nurse that we would learn about a couple of years later? Maybe it was an appearance by Dr. Fridel himself? We may never have the answers to such questions. Whomever it was, I am glad they stopped by to say, "Hello."

12

The Mediums

"I suspect everybody has a degree of psychic ability, just as everybody has a degree of athletic or artistic ability. Some people have special gifts; other people have a particular interest that leads them to develop their abilities. But the phenomenon itself is ordinary and widespread."

— Michael Crichton,

THIS BOOK WOULD NOT BE COMPLETE without a section devoted to our experiences with mediums and sensitives attending our tour. The stories included throughout this book have been shared by individuals who were completely unaware of ghostly activity until they had an experience. There were so many reports by sensitives we felt obligated to dedicate a section to those who shared their impressions with us.

THEY WALK AMONG US

There are believers, skeptics, and those who will always be nonbelievers when it comes to mediums. Suffice to say, experiences with trustworthy mediums through attendance of many private, group, and personal readings our team are now supporters of the psychic community. Through personal experience it would not surprise me if 25% of the population are sensitive to the paranormal. We all possess a sixth sense, intuition, or gut feeling about circumstances, but others have extremely heightened skills. I am not one of these individuals. I have a great amount of experience regarding parapsychology, or the study of psychic phenomenon. Those with these talents see them as a harsh burden that interferes with their daily life.

There are many mediums and psychics walking around living seemly normal lives when inside there is little resemblance to what most of us consider normal. Our team has worked with this group for so long we easily distinguish the rock stars from the groupies. We give a certain level of trust to someone's reported impressions. Bearing in mind unless it is specific or repeatedly reported by various individuals then we don't take most reports at face value.

No one stands to gain anything by being 'outed' as having psychic abilities. If their secret ever gets out, they are criticized or laughed at. Here in the south there is a large community of Baptist followers who harbor a harsh stigma about those who claim to be mediums. Those earning a living do so knowing they can never 'clock out' because once the doors are opened you will be constantly bombarded with spirit energy. Usually encounters occur at the most inappropriate of times, when the mind is relaxing, and the skilled doesn't have his or her guard up. Often, spirit comes to them when they are falling asleep at night or washing their hair in the shower. It is not an easy life. I've been told countless times that when spirit wants to be heard, it will be heard. The only way to satisfy energies from persistent nagging is to deliver the message that needs to be delivered and it must be delivered to the right person.

Using Mediums as an Investigative Tool: Our Introduction

A few months into investigating and the thought of using a medium to help gather evidence never crossed our minds. A highly unlikely meeting with someone I had gone to school with, from kindergarten to graduation, came into our lives. She had, as had many like her, kept her abilities close being cautioned by good old Southern doctrine that you "just don't talk about those things." Her entire maternal family had abilities, but they did not speak of them. The family were all devout Baptists and it was against the doctrine of the Bible, so she had kept quiet about her skills. Curious about her abilities, she joined us on investigations, and using research, electronic surveillance, and witnesses' testimony we were able to compare her impressions. Every time her abilities were consistently validated. We made a point not to share any details, no matter how slight, prior to introducing her to our favorite haunted location.

Since then, we have developed personal and professional relationships with numerous gifted mediums. Mediums we work with are peer-reviewed, background checked, and approved by providing readings by every team member and trusted friends of the team.

Our team must feel confident in their honesty and integrity. Impressions they receive are used against measurements taken by our tools and the detailed stories of our witnesses. This group has proven to be a reliable tool just like any others we may use on investigations.

People know that paranormal investigators are open to hearing their stories. These are the stories and secrets they cannot share with the rest of the world. Most are comfortable we grant them automatic acceptance and confidentiality. It is our job to hear about the bizarre, unusual, and unexplained. We take that responsibility very seriously and we take an objective, non-biased approach to everything they share. Not surprisingly, every tour we offered, at least one person told us about having skills. Some were able to feel, see, hear, taste, and smell other worldly things. In every instance, these individuals received some sort of impressions others simply could not. At times, individuals would talk to us about having clairvoyance, such as dreaming of events so vividly they were almost real, only to have the experience in the following days. Most were truthful about their abilities. Others were truthful but may have exaggerated the skill a bit.

THE ACCIDENTAL OUIJA BOARD TEST

It was pure accident we stumbled on a test to many of their claims. A close friend gave me a Ouija board she found. In a tongue and cheek manner, we created a display on the wall framed by a shadow box. A few "sensitive" guests would talk about its history as soon as they saw it. Some claimed it had been a catalyst for malevolent energies and would provide a brief, vague history of the display. The tales they spoke of were always much more fascinating than the actual truth. The board was a gag that was given to a strict Southern Baptist couple who wanted nothing to do with it. Never opened it was tossed into the attic destined to rot away with other storage items. After the couple passed and the old home was being cleaned out the board was pulled out and thrown behind their bedroom door. Hearing horror stories about Ouija boards, the adult children opened it but soon threw it behind the bedroom door not knowing what to do with it. The strict religious upbringing had absolutely forbidden such "tools of evil." The board, being exposed to wet, damp, dark conditions gave it a fantastic look of antiquity. This Ouija board was one of the commonly purchased Parker Brother's games sold in the

1980's.

Unseen Eyes Watching Our Tour

Our tour guides were sometimes overwhelmed with stories from sensitives on the tour that aligned with stories from others. These stories came from people who often had nothing to gain from sharing. We gathered impressions from children as young as 14, stories from fire fighters and other civil servants, men and women, and some of the most unlikely people you could imagine. The stories were always whispering in the ears of the tour guides and were never speaking aloud in public.

Alley Street in Terrell runs parallel and adjacent to the railroad. When the city was beginning its relationship with the railroad, businesses sprang up on both sides of the railroad track. There were saloons, print shops, the newspaper and hardware stores on both sides. One such block, referred to as the "Star Block" began at S. Virginia Street and ran West on the South side of the railroad track, Grove Avenue. A fire began in one of the businesses, with a variety of stories as to its' origin, and the businesses on the South side of the railroad burned. There were no fatalities, but as a result, the businesses on the North side of the tracks turned their attentions to

Moore Avenue. Over the years, entrances facing South to the track were bricked up and the North Moore Avenue entrances became the front of the stores. There are still many of these bricked up entries and windows apparent as you drive Alley Street from S. Virginia to Rockwall Ave. There is even a chained supported awning hanging from one of the stores. Some of these buildings are circa 1880's. Mediums have told us that as we walked that route on the ghost walk West to Books and Crannies, spirits watched from the doorways and windows, waving, excited to be talked about and acknowledged! Upon crossing S. Frances Avenue, the Bass-Rutledge Drug Store's rear wall is exposed, made up of old brick. Apparently there is a "cowboy," decked out in jeans, plaid shirt, and big hat, who leans against that wall, smoking, as he observes the curiosity seekers heading for the back door of Books and Crannies. We don't know if he belongs to one of the existing buildings, or perhaps to the saddle shop that occupied that corner in the 1880's.

Another instance of being watched by Spirits happened at the Old City Hall on N. Adelaide Street. Multiple mediums shared their visions of Spirits standing on the roof, lined up along the two storied front visages, watching the ghost walk guests. I wonder if they were shaking their heads at the tour guide's stories, maybe even calling out from above, wanting to correct our version of events!

MEDIUM IMPRESSIONS IN TERRELL'S HAUNTED BUILDINGS

Over a period, we hosted events in the Iris Theatre in the back of Books and Crannies. The heaviness felt by some upon entering the black box theatre was multiplied by some of the mediums who spent time in the building. One such medium complained at her first visit to the bookstore that there was an angry male spirit in the store, prone to yelling into her ear. After a few such visits, she revealed the reason for his anger. He felt trapped there in the bookstore, and he didn't know how to read!

The Carnegie Library is at the top of the mediums' revelations. We know the building is very active with spirits without confirmation from these gifted folks. However, they have a variety of other impressions. I asked one frequent visitor to the museum why she always moved her chair to the rear of the room during meetings, away from the foyer entrance. She admitted to being sensitive, and explained she was not comfortable in the middle of the room, exposed to the foyer's open double doors. Apparently, there was activity there that distracted her. Other mediums shared being overcome with nausea upon entering the foyer, either from the front doors or having entered through the rear library door. They did not describe a dark or evil presence, just an immense, sweeping energy. Indeed, many of the paranormal experiences in this building revolve around that foyer with its two sweeping staircases to the common landing, and the open auditorium on the second floor. Another medium described the presence of a matronly woman in a rocking chair just outside the ladies' room, at the front South side of the first floor. Another medium feels the presence of the head librarian, shushing and straightening books. The building was a library from its' construction in 1904 until the mid-1980s, so it only stands to reason there's at least one such devoted spirit, happily lingering among the stacks. In fact, all the spirits were content, even happy, and always glad for company from the "other side."

Mediums Abound at the Headquarters

While our headquarters were in a portion of the adjacent building East of the Brin Opera House, we had numerous guests and colleagues sharing their psychic impressions of the building, constructed in the early to mid-1880s.

The original enormous Brin Store safe had been moved to that building and held court over our office space. You've already read about some of the mediums' stories related to this safe. Mr. Brin's presence was all over and all around the safe. Mediums told us there was a stream of people (Spirits!) coming into the front and back doors, walking back and forth. It was a busy spot, apparently. One such person said the Spirits knew she was there and had lined up outside the back door, waiting their turn to be recognized by her so they might send a loved one a message. The place was almost overwhelming for some. One evening after a private ghost walk for a group of Boy Scouts, I was giving a presentation to the group while standing in front of the safe. I noticed a parent with the group looking as if she wanted to break out laughing. Now, we enjoyed ourselves there, but this was a serious talk to a group of young boys about the pros and cons of owning your own business. Later as the group left, the lady pulled me aside and said she could see a woman standing behind me, waving her arms, having a good old time at my expense as I tried to deliver my message. That was a relief, and I have no doubt the spirits there made fun of us on more than one occasion.

One day while attending the office, a lady with her young daughter came through the front office, seeking us out. Her daughter appeared to be about 14 years old, soft spoken but serious. She had heard some of the ghost stories being shared on the Terrell Ghost Walk and wanted to share her personal experiences with the young girl spirit we referred to as "Lizzie." She explained that she was sensitive, and that this young spirit had been coming to her in her dreams since she was about five years old. She shared that the child's name was actually "Lissie," and that she died by drowning. Each time the spirit child came to her, her long dark hair was always wet. This family lived in a community near Terrell and did not have long family ties with the town. Perhaps she was seeking this child medium out to share her story with, just as children are drawn to each other in life. Another medium who was a colleague sensed that the young spirit had been the illegitimate daughter of one of the many prostitutes working in the "billiard halls" lining Moore Avenue in the 1800's, and had been left to her own resources most of the time. Whatever the truth, engaged mediums agreed that "Lizzie" or "Lissie" still plays on the sidewalks and in the businesses along Moore Ave.

A Picture Finds Its Home

On another occasion a medium visited us at the office and explained she had encountered a framed portrait, a graphite painting, at a resale shop in a nearby town. This portrait drew her to it, and she believed that its' purpose in attracting her was to help find its' way back to Terrell. She explained that we'd just know it when we saw it. She was reluctant to purchase the portrait and take it home, afraid the spirit would become a permanent resident at her home. Well, that was an easy find, as I flipped through framed paintings of all sorts a few days later at the resale shop. The attractive regal figure was there, high necked blouse, hair swept up and secured with a fancy comb. There was no artist's signature, but simply "J. Newman" written across the back. We settled the portrait into our office space, and with the magical tools of the internet believe we have identified this woman from Terrell as Josephine (Mollie) Newman. She and her husband are buried in the Oakland Cemetery in Terrell. Although our office is no longer in Terrell, we still have the portrait, and some day perhaps we will return it to her extended family.

Working with these individuals has given us a profound respect for their gifts. Their gifts are not easily carried, nor lightly shared. However, I recommend looking around at the audience in the theatre, the other diners in the restaurant, the person in the car beside you at the red light. These gifted folks are all around us, yet only a few shares their secrets. So, yes, we believe.

13

CONCLUSION

"I believe humans have souls, and I believe in the conservation of souls."

-John Green, The Fault in Our Stars

TERRELL'S DOWNTOWN SMALL BUSINESS DISTRICT isn't so much glitter and lights as it once was. However, after the shop owners have closed for the day, this section of Moore Avenue is quiet. The city streets lack pedestrians, except for the occasional person taking the dog for an evening walk. The marquee of the Iris Theatre is lit. This grand monument never sleeps. It is a nightly reminder, full of grandeur, of the blood, sweat, and tears given to small businesses every day. Moore Avenue is a place where the American dream still happens. Every morning when the marquee is dark, owners are getting out of bed and turning the open signs on to invite you in.

Today, you can buy anything online without even putting on your shoes. However, you miss the experience of being there. You can't thumb through a book and feel its pages between your fingers. You miss the slightly musty smell of the resale shop where you may discover a wonder that was somehow put there just for you. You miss out on the small things such as Kit and Kat, the two ceramic cats, gifted to the bookstore owned by her and her husband and sit atop the Iris marquee. If those kittens could talk, they would have stories about that little stretch of avenue no one else knows.

The predecessors of these buildings may have had different items for sale or offer various services, but they are still present in the stone walls of these gloriously beautiful buildings. I tell their stories, so they are not forgotten. They have a legacy there, and I believe they try to share their presence through these ghostly experiences.

When I began my adventure of "Ghost Hunting," I did it because I had questions about the afterlife. There was a thrill in trying to have an experience. That is how most of the paranormal investigators get started. Anyone can go on a search to have a brush with a spirit. There is no shame in wanting to get confirmation with the other side. Just keep in mind, ghosts are people too. Their lack of a physical body doesn't mean that you have permission to be invasive or rude. Treat the departed with respect and dignity. You are now in their territory, and you are the guest. Tread with courtesy and always ask permission. You may never get that confirmation and give up quickly. You may have experiences and decide that was all you needed to prove to yourself the supernatural exists. There are very few that truly dedicate themselves to the hard work, commitment, and patience to become a paranormal researcher. Those that decide to continue the quest to reach the dead do so for the respect of the science and to help others understand what may be happening in their homes by providing education to eliminate fear.

Whether the spirits you seek out haunt Terrell or any other town in the world, remember that you are a visitor and you should act accordingly. Take off your hat, be sure to introduce yourself, and be a good steward. Get permission to enter the premises. Remember, when you speak in a haunted location, the deceased CAN hear you. For God's sake, act like your mama taught you. Come and go with love. If they choose to make themselves known, be grateful for that. You are one of the fortunate.

If you have an opportunity to visit Terrell, tell them we sent you and say, "Hello" for us.

THE IRIS THEATRE MARQUEE

WORKS CITED

Alexander, John. *Ghosts! Washington Revisited: The Ghostlore of the Nation's Capital.* Body, Mind, Spirit, 1998. Book.

Bray, Libba. *Lair of Dreams.* n.d.

Crichton, Michael. *Travels.* Harper Pen, 1988. Book. 22 July 22019. <https://www.amazon.com>.

Emerson, Ralph Waldo. "The Young American." *The Complete Works.* Vol. 12. Boston: Mifflin and Company, 7 February 1844. Lecture read before the Mercantile Library Association.

Eno, Paul F. *Face at the Window: First-Hand Accounts of the Paranormal in South New England.* Second Edition. Woonsocket: New River Press, 1998. Book.

Green, John. *The Fault in Our Stars.* New York: Button Books, 2012. Book.

Heinlein, Robert A. *Time Enough for Love.* First Edition. G.P. Putnam's Sons, 1973. Book: Science Fiction.

Indiana, Logansport Pharos. "Terrell, Texas Awning Collapse, Nov 1984." 5 November 1894.

GenDisasters. Ed. Stu Beitler. Online Contributor. 16 June 2019. <GenDisasters.com>.

McCarty, Louis P. "Statistician and Economist." *The Book Trade Generally* 7th September 1898, 19th Publication ed.: 691. Online Article in Periodical. 3 November 2019. <https://books.googleusercontent.com>.

Riordan, Rick. *The Throne of Fire (The Kane Chronicles Book 2)*. Vol. 2. Penguin Books Limited, 2011. Graphic Novel.

The New York Times. "Terrell, TX Awning Collapse, Nov 1894." 4 November 1894. *GenDisasters.com*. Ed. Stu Beitler. The New York Times. Online Contributor. 16 June 2019.

Welles, Orson. *Orson Welles Quotes and Phrases*. 2011-2019. Quotation Collection. 13 June 2019. <https://quote-citation.com>.

Wikipedia. *Carnegie Library*. 2019. Community Driven Wiki. 4 June 2019. <https://en.wikipedia.org>.

Willowmoon, Lianne. *Soul Antiquary*. Plano: Hydra Productions, 2018. Book.

XIV, Dalai Lama. *Best Dalai Lama Quotes*. Ed. Unlisted Author. 2016. Quotation Collection Online. 13 June 2019. <https://www.bestdalailamaquotes.com>.

Yovanoff, Brenna. "Good Reads." n.d. *Brenna Yovanoff, Quotes, Quotable Quote.* Online Quotation Collection. 3 November 2018. <https://www.goodreads.com>.

ACKNOWLEDGMENTS

Amy: You taught me to step outside of my comfort zone, no matter how difficult. You brought me closer to God. It is because of you I don't just believe, but I KNOW.

Morgan, Mitzi, & Barbara Miller: Your blind support and faith will never be forgotten.

Desiree: You are a true servant leader. I am a better person for knowing you.

The business owners of Terrell and the Chamber of Commerce: Thank you for your trust in sharing your stories. It has been an honor to represent you and the predecessors who came before.

Third Dimension Paranormal: Your mentorship was priceless. We will always strive to emulate the professionalism your team demonstrates.

Those who stepped in to help when we needed it: You helped share your passion through your deeds. You are family not by blood but love.

Those who kicked us in the teeth: You gave us focus to get it right. Neither of us was perfect in actions nor deeds. If there is a passion, there is progress regardless of what side you are on

ABOUT THE AUTHOR

Brenda is one of the co-founders of the paranormal team, S.P.I.R.I.T. and has conducted hundreds of hours of investigation at highly active locations. Brenda is completing her studies as a field investigator for the Mutual UFO Network, is proficient in the study of electronic voice phenomenon, and works closely with mediums. She holds a general membership at the Rhine Research Center (Duke University), the longest running research program dedicated to studying parapsychology, trying to understand the science behind psychic ability. Brenda holds a business degree from the University of Phoenix and holds several certifications in online digital marketing.

Brenda's personal exploration focuses on the latest theories of paranormal science and understanding the psychology of belief. As well, she has classroom and online training in critical thinking. She recently completed an online course in and the application of skepticism. She has diverse practical experience in investigation techniques including client interviewing, planning and preparation, conducting and documenting control studies, EVP analysis, videography, and facilitating the team's medium during location readings.

She and her team have been featured on the popular radio show, Texas Road Trippin' with J. D. Ryan, Ride Texas Magazine (a publication of Texas Monthly) and was a cover feature of Kaufman County Times.

Brenda is the founder and developer of the Terrell Ghost Walk, developing a trustworthy and skilled Medium program including private, group, and gallery readings, and has written several educational programs including dealing with malevolent energies and how to conduct and analyze electronic voice phenomenon.

Brenda lives in east Texas with her husband, her three dogs. Although, she is currently recovering from a spinal injury when able she enjoys defensive competition shooting, gardening, and spending time with friends and family.

THE CO-AUTHOR

After a 30-year career of government service, Mary Jo developed diligence in paying attention to detail and provided the grooming for a no-nonsense approach to investigating the paranormal. A life-long artist and hobby photographer, she sees details in objects with a precision provided from years of practical experience.

Mary Jo relies on a Samsung NX2000 for investigative photography. Mary Jo has invested countless hours of personal research into the multi-faceted approaches of the photographic documentation of haunted locations. She possesses an uncanny ability to analyze photographs, identifying issues resulting in misidentified anomalies. Mary Jo has been successful in capturing the likeness of many ghostly figures.

She has always had an interest in the paranormal, having her first personal experience at the age of 12. After capturing a ghostly apparition on film in 2012 she and her family established S.P.I.R.I.T., a paranormal team in Dallas, TX. Hundreds of hours have gone into the experimentation, research, and documentation of profoundly haunted locations by her and her team. She has participated in all aspects of the paranormal process, including conducting control studies, planning and executing investigations, working with medium evidence, EVP analysis, video analysis, and historical data research. Although she spends the most time working with spirits and ghosts, she has a diverse background in all aspects of the paranormal. Her other research includes parapsychology, cryptozoology, and ufology. She is a blogger and often a podcast guest for dallasghosts.com.

Mary Jo has also developed training programs in photography for paranormal investigations, and the introduction to paranormal investigations. She and her team have been featured on radio show, Texas Road Trippin' with J.D. Ryan, Ride Texas Magazine (a publication of Texas Monthly), and on the cover of Kaufman County Times.

Mary Jo lives in North Central Texas with her husband and her dog, Buddy. She enjoys gardening and painting, but most of all, investigating and educating others in all aspects of the paranormal. She is currently studying the art of reading tarot cards.

www.ingramcontent.com/pod-product-compliance
Lightning Source LLC
Chambersburg PA
CBHW051024030426
42336CB00015B/2713

* 9 7 8 1 7 3 3 7 4 1 0 0 2 *